Selected Songs
for Voice and Piano

ERNEST CHAUSSON

Selected and edited by
Victor Rangel-Ribeiro

DOVER PUBLICATIONS, INC.
Mineola, New York

Copyright

Published in Canada by General Publishing Company, Ltd., 30 Lesmill Road, Don Mills, Toronto, Ontario.
Published in the United Kingdom by Constable and Company, Ltd., 3 The Lanchesters, 162–164 Fulham Palace Road, London W6 9ER.

Bibliographical Note

This Dover publication, first published in 1998, is a new compilation of songs originally published separately. J. Hamelle, Paris, originally published the following songs individually, under the group title *Mélodies pour Chant et Piano par Ernest Chausson:* "Nanny," "Les Papillons," "Sérénade italienne," "La Cigale" and "La Caravane," all n.d. A. Durand et Fils, Paris, originally published "Chanson perpétuelle," n.d. Together with a reprint of "Chanson perpétuelle," the nineteen additional songs in the Dover collection were published together by Rouart, Lerolle & Cie, Paris, in *Ernest Chausson, Vingt Mélodies,* 1910.

The introduction, glossary and English translations of the French poems were specially prepared for this edition by Victor Rangel-Ribeiro. The annotated contents list and main headings are newly added.

International Standard Book Number: 0-486-40415-3

Manufactured in the United States of America
Dover Publications, Inc., 31 East 2nd Street, Mineola, N.Y. 11501

Chausson's *Mélodies*

In his sixteen active years as a composer, Ernest Chausson wrote forty-one *mélodies,* thirty-five of which were published. While the composer's popular *Poème* for violin and orchestra and *Concerto for violin, piano, and string quartet* have both buried the *mélodies* in their shadow, Chausson's beautifully crafted songs are at least as significant as any of his other compositions.

To English speakers, the term *mélodie* itself can be misleading. In the context of French art song, its true meaning is that the text is the decisive element, out of which the melody emerges. While the same may be said for contemporary songs composed to texts in other languages, French composers face a unique problem in that rhythm in French poetry depends on 'quantity'—that is, the duration of a particular vowel or syllable—rather than on accent, affecting musical phrasing in subtle ways.

Chausson invariably sought to sculpt the music to fit the text. With some of Maurice Maeterlinck's poems—*Serre chaude* comes to mind—the texture becomes dense to match the poet's obscure meanings; elsewhere, as in *Les Papillons,* the texture can be flowing and airy. Here and there one comes across the strong influences that affected Chausson's creative processes—César Franck, his private composition teacher for a good three years; and Richard Wagner, whose "Tristan chord" (a combination of two fourths, one augmented and the other perfect) color so many of the Chausson *mélodies,* including *La Caravane.* Moussorgsky's hand can be seen in *Lassitude.*

Chausson, somewhat melancholic by nature, reveals himself in his choice of text. Most deal with love—love lost forever, love gone sour, but fortunately also idyllic love, love fondly remembered, love exalted. His first song was *Nanny*; his last, the *Chanson perpétuelle.* Both deal with a lost love; in the final song, with abandonment. They frame the twenty-five songs included in this volume.

These include settings of Maurice Bouchor's original poems, as well as his translations of songs from Shakespeare's plays. The latter are free renderings, providing at once rather more and far less than Shakespeare managed to convey in his terse originals. Leconte de Lisle, whose poems Chausson also set, belonged to the French school of "Parnassian" poets; we are indeed transported to Parnassus when Zeus, Apollo, other ancient gods and the Attic sun are invoked in praise of the humble cicada.

Most strongly represented are the Symbolist poets—such men as Mauclair, Maeterlinck, Moréas, and Verlaine—who lived at once in two worlds: one, the turn-of-the-century world of lassitude, ennui, despair, and decadence; the other, the wild world of their imaginings.

Maeterlinck's poems, by their very abstruseness and disjointedness, demanded special treatment, both from Chausson and from this translator. The musicologist W. D. Halls describes these poems as being written by "a mind at the end of its tether and . . . near to dementia." In deciphering Maeterlinck's tortured phrases, I sought solace and advice from my friend William Warner, a linguist who revels in French literature. Bill, clueing me in to the nuances within nuances that are at once the glory of French poetry and the bane of all translators, now receives my thanks.

Victor Rangel-Ribeiro

Glossary

augmentez un peu = *poco crescendo*

au (premier) mouvement [mouv^t] = *a tempo (I)*

calme, calm, even

doux, gentle, sweet, smooth

en animant et en augmentant, becoming livelier and louder

en augmentant (un peu), becoming (a little) louder

en diminuant (jusqu'à la fin), gradually softer (until the end)

en pressant (un peu), rushing (a little)

en ralentissant (beaucoup) = *(molto) rallentando*

en retenant (beaucoup), (greatly) holding back

en revenant au 1er mouv^t, gradually returning to the main tempo

expressif, expressive

gaiement, gaily

large, broad

lentement, slowly

lent (et triste) (et résigné), slow (and sad)(and resigned)

m.d. [main droite], right hand

m.g. [main gauche], left hand

modéré, moderate

moins, less

mouvementé, moving along

pas (trop) vite, not (too) fast

plus, more

plus animé, livelier

plus ***f***, louder

plus lent (grave), slower (somber)

plus vite, faster

[première] Ier mouv^t [mouvement] = Tempo I

retenu, held back

sans hâte, unrushed

sans lenteur, moving along without undue slowness

sans ralentir = *non rallentando*

simplement, simply

toujours = *sempre,* always

très = *molto,* very

— *calme,* very calm

— *doux,* very gentle, sweet, smooth

— *égal et sans nuances,* very even and unshaded

— *leger* = *molto leggiero*

— *lent,* very slow

— *modérément animé,* very moderately animated

— *(peu) retenu,* very (slightly) held back

— *simple,* very simple, unaffected

un peu moins lent, not quite as slow

un peu plus fort, a little louder

un peu retenu, slightly held back

vif, lively

Contents

Dates of composition appear in parentheses.

Nanny 1
No. 1 (1880) from *Sept mélodies,* Op. 2 • Poem by Leconte de Lisle

Les papillons [Butterflies] 4
No. 3 (1880) from *Sept mélodies,* Op. 2 • Poem by Théophile Gautier

Sérénade italienne [Italian serenade] 8
No. 5 (1880) from *Sept mélodies,* Op. 2 • Poem by Paul Bourget

Nocturne 12
No. 1 (1886) from *Quatre mélodies,* Op. 8 • Poem by Maurice Bouchor

Amour d'antan [To an old love] 16
No. 2 (1882) from *Quatre mélodies,* Op. 8 • Poem by Maurice Bouchor

Printemps triste [Joyless spring] 20
No. 3 (1883) from *Quatre mélodies,* Op. 8 • Poem by Maurice Bouchor

Nos souvenirs [Memories] 26
No. 4 (1888) from *Quatre mélodies,* Op. 8 • Poem by Maurice Bouchor

La cigale [The cicada] 31
No. 4 (1887) from *Quatre mélodies,* Op. 13 • Poem by Leconte de Lisle

La caravane [The caravan] 36
Op. 14 (1887) • Poem by Théophile Gautier

Le temps des lilas [The time of lilacs] 41
Closing section of "La mort de l'amour"—Part 3 of *Poème de l'amour et de la mer,* Op. 19 (1886) • Poem by Maurice Bouchor

Serre chaude [Greenhouse] 46
No. 1 (1896) from *Serres chaudes,* Op. 24 • Poem by Maurice Maeterlinck

Serre d'ennui [Hothouse of ennui] 54
No. 2 (1893) from *Serres chaudes,* Op. 24 • Poem by Maurice Maeterlinck

Lassitude 58
No. 3 (1893) from *Serres chaudes,* Op. 24 • Poem by Maurice Maeterlinck

Fauves las [Wearied beasts] 62
No. 4 (1896) from *Serres chaudes,* Op. 24 • Poem by Maurice Maeterlinck

Oraison [A prayer] 67
No. 5 (1895) from *Serres chaudes,* Op. 24 • Poem by Maurice Maeterlinck

Les heures [The hours]. 70
No. 1 (1896) from *Trois lieder,* Op. 27 • Poem by Camille Mauclair

Ballade. 73
No. 2 (1896) from *Trois lieder,* Op. 27 • Poem by Camille Mauclair

Les couronnes [Garlands]. 77
No. 3 (1896) from *Trois lieder,* Op. 27 • Poem by Camille Mauclair

Chanson de clowns [Song of the clowns] 80
No. 1 (1890) from *Chansons de Shakespeare,* Op. 28 •
Text by Maurice Bouchor, based on "Come away, come away, death"
from William Shakespeare's *Twelfth Night,* Act II, Scene iv

Chanson d'amour [Song of love] 84
No. 2 (1891) from *Chansons de Shakespeare,* Op. 28 •
Text by Maurice Bouchor, based on "Take, O! take those lips away"
from William Shakespeare's *Measure for Measure,* Act IV, Scene i

Chanson d'Ophélia [Ophelia's song]. 88
No. 3 (1896) from *Chansons de Shakespeare,* Op. 28 •
Text by Maurice Bouchor, based on "He is dead and gone, lady"
from William Shakespeare's *Hamlet,* Act IV, Scene v

La chanson bien douce [A very sweet song] 90
No. 1 (1910) from *Deux poèmes,* Op. 34 • Poem by Paul Verlaine

Cantique à l'épouse [A canticle for the wife] 97
No. 1 (1896) from *Deux mélodies,* Op. 36 • Poem by Albert Jounet

Dans la forêt du charme et de l'enchantement
[In the forest of charm and enchantment] 102
No. 2 (1898) from *Deux mélodies,* Op. 36 • Poem by Jean Moréas

Chanson perpétuelle [Perpetual chanson] 109
Op. 37 (1898) • Poem by Charles Cros
[Piano part transcribed by the composer from the orchestral original]

Text Translations
by Victor Rangel-Ribeiro

Nanny
[Leconte de Lisle]

Woods dear to the pigeons, weep, sweet foliage,
And you, lively spring, and you, cool paths;
Weep, o wild heather,
Bushes of holly and of wild roses.
Spring, beflowered king of the verdant year,
O young god, weep!
Ripening Summer, cut your crowning locks,
And weep, blushing Autumn.
Love's anguish now wounds a faithful heart.
Earth and sky, weep!
Oh, how I did love her!
Dear countryside, speak of her no more;
Nanny will not return, not ever.

Butterflies
[Théophile Gautier, *Les papillons*]

Butterflies white as snow
Winging in great clouds over the ocean;
Lovely white butterflies, when may I
Take to the blue highways of the sky?

Do you know, loveliest of lovelies,
My jade-eyed dancing girl—
If they should lend me their wings,
Tell me, do you know where I would go?

Without stealing a kiss from the roses
Across valleys and forests I would fly
To your half-parted lips,
Flower of my being, and I would die.

Italian serenade
[Paul Bourget, *Sérénade italienne*]

Let us sail out in a boat on to the sea
To spend the night beneath the stars.
Look! There's just enough of a breeze
To swell the canvas sail.

The old Italian fisherman
And his two sons, who are our crew,
Listen but understand nothing
Of the words we speak.

On the calm and somber sea, behold!
We can exchange our souls
And none will understand our voices
But the night, and the sky, and the waves.

Nocturne
[Maurice Bouchor]

The night was brooding and dark; only
A few golden pins glittered
In her long black tresses
That over us—over the distant seas and the earth,
Wrapped in a sleep fraught with mystery—
Spread winged perfume.

And our young love, born of our thoughts,
Began to waken on a bed of a hundred icy roses
That had breathed no more than a day;
And I, I said to her, pale and trembling with fever,
That we would die as one, a smile upon our lips,
At the same moment as our love.

To an old love
[Maurice Bouchor, *Amour d'antan*]

My love from days gone by, do you remember?
Fed by sweet kisses, our hearts bloomed
Like two roses in a spring wind.
Do you remember these things of the past?

In your golden dreams do you forever see
Blue horizons, and the sunny sea
That kisses your feet while falling languidly asleep?
In your golden dreams, do you perhaps forget?

In the pale light of Aprils past,
Do you feel the flower of your dreams unfolding,
A bouquet of fresh and fragrant thoughts?
Lovely Aprils, spent down there, on the shore!

Joyless spring
[Maurice Bouchor, *Printemps triste*]

Our beloved paths have bloomed again,
But my broken heart cannot be mended.
Thus each evening do I run
To weep and weep beneath your window,

Your empty window, where no longer shines
Your delightful head nor your sweet smile.
As I think back on our lost days
I grieve, and I know not what to say.

And the flowers always, and always the sky
And the spirit of the woods in deep shade
Murmur in chorus an eternal chant
That wafts through the enraptured air.

And the sea that rolls towards the rising sun
Carrying my thoughts far away . . .
If only, on the wings of the wind,
My thoughts could fly to you, those wounded doves!

Memories
[Maurice Bouchor, *Nos souvenirs*]

Our memories—all the things
That we scatter to the winds
Like rose petals
Or the wings of butterflies—
Retain the secret fragrance
Of a joy long gone.
Isn't it amazing
How the past reappears?

At certain moments it seems
The dream will last forever,
And that we are again united
As in the time of our lost love.

While we, falling asleep,
Are lulled by the half-heard song
Of a voice that charms the ear,
A name springs to our lips

And this hour when we remember
How freely our hearts were surrendered
Is like a beating of wings
Returning from a joyous past.

The cicada
[Leconte de Lisle, *La cigale*]

O cicada, born when the days turn fine,
Poised on green boughs at the crack of dawn,
Happy to sip a droplet of dew—
Like a king, you sing incessantly.

Innocent in all things, gentle and free from guile,
The happy farmer, sheltered by an oak,
Hears you from afar announcing summer.
Apollo honors you as he honors the Muses,
And Zeus has granted you immortality.

Hail, wise child of the ancient earth,
Whose song is an invitation to sleep,
And who, under the rays of the Attic sun,
Having neither flesh nor blood, are akin to the gods.

The caravan
[Théophile Gautier, *La caravane*]

The human caravan, in the Sahara that is the world,
Through the trail of years from which there is no return
Go dragging their feet, burned by the fires of the day,
And licking the sweat that pours down their arms.

The great lion roars, and a tempest glowers;
On the fleeing horizon there's neither minaret nor tower.
The only shade's the shadow cast by a vulture
Sweeping the skies, searching for its rotten prey.

They plod on, and on, and then they espy
Some trace of green they point out to one another,
A clump of cypress trees littered with white headstones.

For your rest, God in the desert of time
Has strewn the oases of cemeteries.
Lie down and sleep, o panting travelers!

The time of lilacs
[Maurice Bouchor, *Le temps des lilas*]

The time of lilacs and the time of roses
Will not come back again this spring;
The time of lilacs and the time of roses
Has passed; the time of carnations as well.

The wind has changed, the skies have turned gloomy,
No more will we run to cull
The lilacs in bloom and the lovely roses;
The spring is joyless and cannot flower.

O joyful and sweet springtime
That, last year, brought sunshine into our lives!
Our flower of love has faded.
Alas, that your kisses can no longer revive it!

And you, what do you do, now? No flowers bloom,
There's neither joyful sunshine nor cooling shade.
The time of lilacs and the time of roses,
Together with our love, is forever dead.

Greenhouse
[Maurice Maeterlinck, *Serre chaude*]

O greenhouse that resembles a forest!
Your doors forever closed
On everything that lies beneath your dome!
In my soul I find analogies!

The thoughts of a hungry princess,
The boredom of a sailor in the desert;
Brass music beneath the windows of the incurably ill.
Get thee to the coolest corners!

One would say a woman fainted one harvest day;
There are postillions in the courtyard of a hospice.
Far off, an elk hunter turned nurse passes by.
Examine her by moonlight!

Oh! Nothing is in its place.
One would say a madwoman is facing the judges;
A warship under full sail
Rides a canal.

Some night birds roost on the lilies
A bell tolls around noon. (There beneath the bells!)
A stopping place for the sick on the prairie,
The smell of ether on a sunny day.

My God! My God!
When will we have the rain
And the snow
And the wind in the greenhouse!

Hothouse of ennui
[Maurice Maeterlinck, *Serre d'ennui*]

Oh, this blue boredom in my heart!
Seen more clearly
In the weeping moonlight
My dreams, blue with languor!

This ennui blue as a hothouse
Where one sees enclosed, through
Deep green panes
Covered by moon and glass
Great vegetations
Where the forgotten nightbird lies down
Immobile
Like a dream
On the roses of passion;
Where the water slowly rises
Blurring moon and sky
In a mournful eternal sob
Monotonously as in a dream.

Lassitude

[Maurice Maeterlinck]

They no longer know where to plant their kisses,
Lips pressed to eyes that are blind and cold;
From now on asleep in their splendid dream
They gaze entranced as dogs in the field
Might watch a flock of grey sheep on the horizon
Grazing the moonlight scattered on the grass,
Indifferent to the sky's caresses, vague as is their life,
And without a trace of desire
For the joyous roses blooming beneath their feet
And this long newfound peace they do not comprehend.

Wearied beasts

[Maurice Maeterlinck, *Fauves las*]

Oh the passions in the boulevards
And the laughter and the sobs!
Lying sick and heavy-lidded
Amid the fallen leaves,
The yellow dogs of my sins,
The false hyenas of my hatreds
And on the pallid boredom of the plains
The lions of love are resting!

In the powerlessness of their dream
And languid beneath the languor
Of their mournful, colorless sky,
They endlessly watch
The sheep of temptation
Slowly recede, one by one,
In the stillness of the moonlight,
My immobile passions!

A prayer

[Maurice Maeterlinck, *Oraison*]

You know, Lord, my misery!
You see that I bring you
Evil flowers from the earth
And a bit of sun on one that is dead;
See, too, my lassitude,
The moon darkened and the dawn black;
Render fertile my solitude
By watering it with your glory.
Open your path to me, Lord.
Enlighten my weary soul
Because sadness covers my joy
As ice would blanket a meadow.

The hours

[Camille Mauclair, *Les heures*]

The pallid hours, in the moonlight
Singing when about to die
With a sad smile,
Go one by one
On a lake bathed in moonlight
Where, with a somber smile
They proffer, one by one,
The hands that will lead to death.
And others, ashen beneath the moon,
With iridescent unsmiling eyes
Knowing that this hour brings death
Give their hands, one by one,
And all go into the shadows and the moonlight
To languish and then die
With the hours, one by one,
The hours of the pallid smile.

Ballade

[Camille Mauclair]

When the angels were lost
Who were coming by sea,
The birds waited for them,
Shrieking frantically
In the bitter wind.

When the ships were lost
That were coming by sea,
The birds waited for them;
Then, they rose in the bitter wind,
They soared all the way to the cottages
That sleep by the edge of the sea;
And they said that the angels were lost,
The angels that had been expected.

They went to the church bell towers
That sing according to the breeze,
And they said that the ships had been lost,
The awaited ships.

And that night strange children
Saw the angels' wings
Like ships floating in the sky,
Saw sails like wings
Gliding towards the stars.

And blending together the wings, the sails,
And the ships and the angels,
The frail children prayed
In a blind ignorance.

Garlands

[Camille Mauclair, *Les couronnes*]

It is the little girl with the rings under her eyes
And the astonished air
And her three flimsy garlands—

One of cool pimpernel,
The other of lacy vines,
And in the third an autumn rose.

The pimpernel is for her soul,
The vine is to amuse herself with,
The rose for the one who will love her.

Brave knight! Brave knight!
But no one passes by any more,
And the young girl with rings under her eyes
Has let her garlands fall.

Song of the clowns

[Maurice Bouchor, *Chanson de clowns*]

Fly, my soul, fly!
I die under the spell of the cruellest of virgins.
Come, o death!
Lay me by candlelight
In a coffin of black cypress.

Bury me far from her
In a pale shroud strewn with yew
That, sharing my fate, a true but tardy friend,
At least will remain faithful.

Let not one flower, one poor flower
Be planted on my tomb!
For me neither friend nor a beloved voice
Should speak words of sorrow.

Leave me alone with my pain
And let the desert bleach my bones,
Lest on my tomb, alas, true lovers
Shed torrents of vain tears.

Original Text

[Shakespeare, *Twelfth Night,* Act II, Scene iv]

Come away, come away, death,
And in sad cypress let me be laid;
Fly away, fly away, breath;
I am slain by a fair cruel maid.

My shroud of white, stuck all with yew,
O! prepare it!
My part of death, no one so true
Did share it.

Not a flower, not a flower sweet,
On my black coffin let there be strown;
Not a friend, not a friend greet
My poor corpse, where my bones shall be thrown:
A thousand thousand sighs to save,
O! lay me, where
Sad true lover never find my grave
To weep there.

Song of love

[Maurice Bouchor, *Chanson d'amour*]

Take far, far from me the lips that I adore,
And whose deceit, alas! yet proved so sweet;
Those lovely eyes that the May sky mistakes for the dawn,
Those eyes that make the morning jealous.
Take far, far from me the lips that I adore,
And whose deceit, alas! yet proved so sweet.

But if, despite all, my pain should touch you,
Ah! then yield, yield to me again my kisses,
Seals of love that were placed in vain
Upon your eyes, your eyes, and your lips.

Original Text

[Shakespeare, *Measure for Measure,* Act IV, Scene i]

Take, O! take those lips away,
That so sweetly were forsworn;
And those eyes, the break of day,
Lights that do mislead the morn:
But my kisses bring again,
Bring again,
Seals of love, but seal'd in vain,
Seal'd in vain.

Ophelia's song

[Maurice Bouchor, *Chanson d'Ophélia*]

He is dead, having suffered enough,
Madame; he has gone; it's a done thing,
A stone at his feet, and green grass
On which to rest his head.
On the blanket of snow, sown freely by the handful,
A thousand perfumed flowers,
Before going down into the earth with him
In the bloom of their youth,
Have drunk, like a fresh rain,
The tears of a true love.

Original Text

[Shakespeare, *Hamlet,* Act IV, Scene v]

He is dead and gone, lady,
He is dead and gone;
At his head a grass-green turf,
At his heels a stone.

White his shroud as the mountain snow,
Larded with sweet flowers;
Which bewept to the grave did go,
With true-love showers.

A very sweet song

[Paul Verlaine, *La chanson bien douce*]

Listen to the very sweet song
That only weeps to please you.
It is discreet and light:
A glint of water on moss.
You knew the voice and loved it,
But now it is veiled
Like a heartbroken widow;
And yet like her it is also proud,
And within the long folds of her veil
That pulse in the autumn breeze
It hides and reveals to an astonished heart
The truth, like a star.
It says, this recognizable voice,
That goodness is our life,
That nothing remains of hate and envy
When death comes.
Listen to the voice that persists
In its naive nuptial song.
Consider, nothing is better for the soul
Than to make another soul less sad.
The soul that suffers without anger
Though in pain is merely passing through.
And as the moral of this is clear—
Listen to the song that is wise indeed.

A canticle for the wife

[Albert Jounet, *Cantique à l'épouse*]

Spouse with the luminous brow,
Now that evening falls
And casts into your eyes
Rays the color of blood.

The enchanted twilight
Surrounds you in a fiery radiance.
Come sing me a song
As lovely as a dark rose;

Or, rather, do not sing,
Come lie upon my heart,
Let me kiss your arms
Pale as the flowering dawn.

The night of your eyes enfolds me,
A tremulous night, mystical
And sweet as your smile,
Happy yet tinged with sadness.

And suddenly the depths
Of the consecrated past,
The mystery and the grandeur
Of our lasting love,

Open up in our inmost thoughts
Like an immense valley
Where neglected forests
Dream in profound silence.

In the forest of charm and enchantment

[Jean Moréas, *Dans la forêt du charme et de l'enchantement*]

Beneath your dark tresses, little fairies,
You sweetly sang along my way
In the forest of charm and enchantment.
In the forest of charm and of marvelous rites,
Caring gnomes, while I slept,
From your hands, honest gnomes, you offered me
A scepter of gold, alas! while I lay sleeping.
I learned later that these are a lure and a delusion,
The golden scepters and the songs in the forest.
Yet, like a credulous child, I weep for them
And I would once again sleep in the forest,
No matter that I know they are a lure and a delusion.

Perpetual chanson

[Charles Cros, *Chanson perpétuelle*]

Rustling forests, starry skies,
My beloved has gone
Carrying with him my desolate heart.

May your plaintive murmurs, O winds,
And your songs, charming nightingales,
Go tell him that I die.

The first evening he came here
My soul was at his mercy;
I knew no pride.

My glances were full of confessions.
He held me in uneasy arms
And kissed me near my hair.

I was greatly thrilled,
And later, I'm not sure how,
He became my lover.

I said to him: "You will love me
For as long as you can."
I did not sleep well except in his arms.

But he, feeling heartbroken,
Left the other morning
Without me to a distant land.

Since I no longer have my friend
I will die in the pond
Among the flowers, under water.

When I reach the edge,
I shall dreamily say his name to the wind,
For there I have often waited for him.

And as if in a golden shroud
In my disheveled hair
I will abandon myself to the whims of the wind.

Past happiness will pour
Its sweet light on my brow
And the green bulrushes will enfold me,

And my trembling breast, at this caress,
Will believe that it is being embraced
By the arms of an absent lover.

Nanny

No. 1 (1880) from *Sept mélodies,* Op. 2 • Poem by Leconte de Lisle

animato.
temps, roi fleu - ri de la ver-te an - né - - e,
Poco animato.
mf
O jeu - ne Dieu, pleu - - re! E - té mûris-
sf
3
cresc.
col 8
sant, cou-pe ta tres - - se cou - ron - né - e; Et pleu - - re, Au-tom -
sf
cresc.
- - ne rou-gis - sant. L'an - gois - se d'ai - mer brise un-
Tempo I.
rit.
mf
cresc.
f
mf
col 8

cœur fi - dè - le. Ter - re et ciel, pleu -
f en retenant
rit.
rez! Oh! Que je l'ai - mais!
f en retenant
rit.
un peu plus lent
p
3
dim.
Cher pa - ys, ne par - le plus d'el - le; Nan -
p un peu plus lent
en retenant
ny ne re - vien - dra ja - mais!
en retenant
pp

Les papillons
[Butterflies]

No. 3 (1880) from *Sept mélodies,* Op. 2 • Poem by Théophile Gautier

blancs; Quand pour - rai - je Pren - dre le
Poco rit.
a Tempo
bleu che - min de l'air?
3
Sa - vez - vous, ô bel - le des bel - - - -
- les, Ma ba - ya - dère aux yeux de jais,

S'ils me vou - laient prê - ter leurs ai - - - -
- les, di - - - - tes, sa - vez - vous
mf
Rit.
Rit.
pp
Rit.
a Tempo
où ji - - rais?
Sans prendre un
Rit.
a Tempo
pp
seul bai - ser aux ro - - - - ses, A tra - vers val -

f
lons et fo - rêts,
J'i - rais à vos
mf
Ritard.
ad libitum
lè - vres mi clo - - - ses,
Fleur de mon
Ritard.
â - me, et j'y mour - rais.
p
pp
ppp

Sérénade italienne

[Italian serenade]

No. 5 (1880) from *Sept mélodies,* Op. 2 • Poem by Paul Bourget

il souf-fle juste as-sez d'air
Pour en-fler la toi-le des voi-les.
Le vieux pê-cheur i-ta-li-en.
Et ses deux fils, qui nous con-dui-sent,
E-cou-tent mais n'en-ten-dent

rien
Aux mots que nos bou-ches se
di - sent.
pp
p
Sur la mer cal-me et som - bre
pp
Vois,
cresc.
dim.
p sans ralentir
Nous pou-vons é-changer nos
p
M.G.

â - - mes,
Et nul ne comprendra nos
M.G.
rit.
mf en ralentissant beaucoup
voix,
Que la nuit, le
rit.
en ralentissant beaucoup
a Tempo
ciel et les la - - - mes.
rit.
M.G.
mf a Tempo
8
p

Nocturne

No. 1 (1886) from *Quatre mélodies,* Op. 8 • Poem by Maurice Bouchor

d'or scin_til_laient dans l'é - bè - ne De ses grands che - veux dé - rou -
- lés, Qui, sur nous, sur la mer lointaine
pp
et sur la terre En_seve - lie en un som - meil plein de mys -
- tè - - re, Se_couaient des par - fums ai -

-lés.
p
Et no-tre jeune a - mour, nais - sant de nos pen -
8
p
-sé - es, S'e-veil - lait sur le lit de cent ro - ses gla -
-cé - es Qui n'a - vaient respi-ré qu'un jour;

mf
cresc.
Et moi, je lui di - sais, pâle et tremblant de
p
cresc.
fiè - vre, Que nous mourrions tous deux, le sou -
un peu moins p
mp
p
- rire à la lè - vre, En mê - me temps
mp
p
que notre a - mour.
re - te - nu
M.G.
pp
pp

Amour d'antan

[To an old love]

No. 2 (1882) from *Quatre mélodies,* Op. 8 • Poem by Maurice Bouchor

doux.
Vous sou-ve-nez-vous de ces
mf
en di - mi -
vieil - les cho - ses?
- nu - ant
pp
mp
Voy - ez - vous tou - jours en vos
p
son - ges d'or
Les ho - ri - zons bleus, la

mer so_leil _ leu - se Qui baisant vos pieds
len - te - ment s'en - dort?
p
En vos songes d'or
mf
p
un peu plus fort
retenu
a Tempo
peut être ou_bli - eu - - se?
retenu
a Tempo
p très doux

en augmentant
p
Au ray - on pâ - li des a - vrils pas - sés Sen_tez -
mp
un peu
vous s'ou - vrir la fleur de vos rê - ves, Bou - quet d'o_do -
3
_rants et de frais pen - sers?
très doux
Beaux a - vrils pas - sés là-bas,
p
pp
sur les grê - ves!
mp
expressif

Printemps triste

[Joyless spring]

No. 3 (1883) from *Quatre mélodies,* Op. 8 • Poem by Maurice Bouchor

p
Aussi chaque
soir me voit ac_courir
Et lon_gue_ment pleu_rer
sous ta fe_
_nê - tre.
Ta fe_nê - tre vide
mf
où ne bril - le plus
Ta tê_te char_mante

et ton doux sou - ri - - re;
Et
p
mf
com_me je pense à nos jours per - dus,
mf
Je me la_men - te,
et je ne sais que
en
di -
di - re.
p
mi
nu
ant

Et tou - jours les fleurs,
et tou - jours le ciel, Et
l'â - me des bois dans leur ombre é - pais - se Mur - mu -
- rant en chœur un chant é - ter - nel Qui se ré -

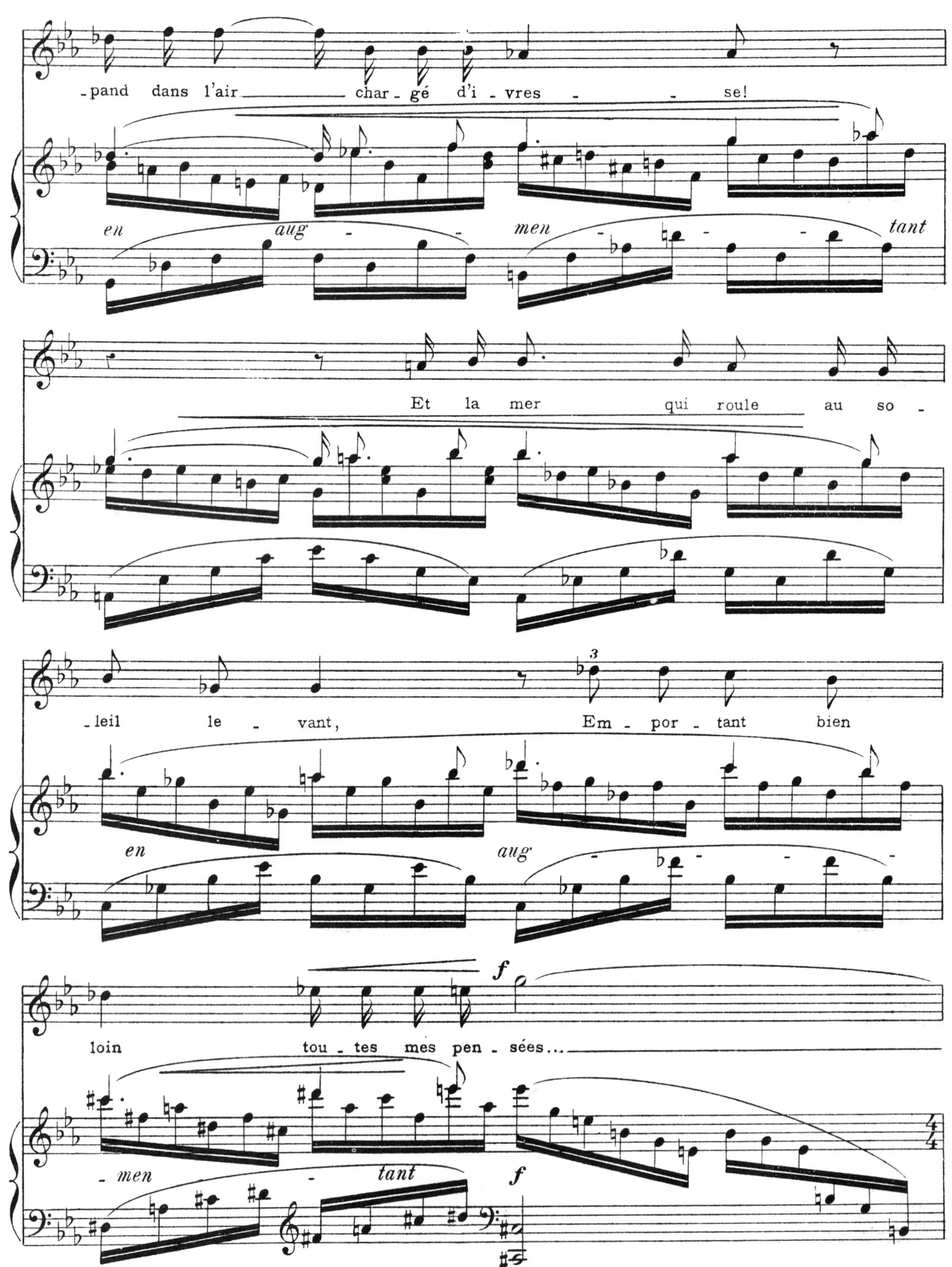
-pand dans l'air charge d'i-vres - - se!
en aug - - men - - - tant
Et la mer qui roule au so-
-leil le - vant, Em - por - tant bien
en aug - - - -
loin tou - tes mes pen - sées...
f
-men - tant
f
3
4
4

moins f
Qu'el-les ail - lent donc sur l'ai - le du vent
Jus-ques à toi, ces co - lom - bes blessées!
retenu

Nos souvenirs

[Memories]

No. 4 (1888) from *Quatre mélodies,* Op. 8 • Poem by Maurice Bouchor

-lons, Ont d'u-ne joie é-va-nou-ie Gar-dé
tout le parfum se-cret,
Et c'est u-ne chose i-nou-
-ïe Comme le pas-sé re-pa-rait.
A de cer-tains mo-ments

il sem_ble Que le rê - ve du - re tou -
-jours Et que l'on soit en_core en - sem - ble
Comme au temps des dé - funts a - mours;
mf
un peu plus lent
pp
poco rit.

Pen - dant qu'a de-mi l'on som-meil - le, Ber -
-cé par la va-gue chan - son D'u-ne voix qui char-me l'o-reil -
-le, Sur les lè - vres vol - tige un nom.
Tempo I°
mf
p Tempo I°
Et cette heure où l'on se rap - pel - le Son cœur fol-le -

-ment dé - pen - sé.
Est comme un fris-son-ne-ment d'ai - -
- le Qui s'en vient du joy - eux pas-sé.
Un peu plus lent
pp
poco cresc.
en re - te - nant
pp
beaucoup
pp

La cigale
[The cicada]

No. 4 (1887) from *Quatre mélodies,* Op. 13 • Poem by Leconte de Lisle

roi, tu chan - - tes tou - jours.
p
m. d.
In-no - cente à tous,
— pai - sible et sans ru - - - - ses,
Le gai la - bou - reur, du chêne a - bri - té.

cresc.
Té _ cou _ _ _ te de loin an_non _
cer l'E _ _ té
f
f
p
A _ pol _ _ lôn t'ho _
p
nore au _ tant que les Mu _ _ _ _ ses.

Et Zeus t'a don - né
rit.
l'Im - mor - ta - li - té!
f a tempo
Sa -
rit.
a tempo
lut, sage en - fant de la terre an -
mf
ti - que, Dont le chant in - vite à
meno f

clo - - - - re les yeux, Et
qui. sous l'ar - deur du so - leil at - - ti - que,
mf
N'ay - ant chair ni sang, vis sem - blable
aux Dieux.
f
f
f

La caravane

[The caravan]

Op. 14 (1887) • Poem by Théophile Gautier

a tempo
va, traînant le pied, brû - lée aux feux du jour,
a tempo
Et buvant sur ses bras la su - eur qui l'i - non - de.
dim.
dim.
dim.
rit.
Plus vite.
mf
Le grand li-on ru git,
a tempo
en pressant
p
mf
et la tem-pê - te gron - de;
A l'hori-
cre - scen - do
f

zon fuyard, ni mi-na-ret, ni tour.
cresc. molto
La seule ombre qu'on ait c'est l'om-bre du vautour qui traverse le ciel,
cresc. molto
cher-chant sa proie im-mon-de.
rit.
a tempo
mf L'on a-van-ce tou-jours, Et voici que l'on
a tempo
f rit.
cresc.
cresc.

voit quelque cho-se de vert que l'on se montre au doigt!
p subito
f
cresc.
ff
Large.
p
C'est un bois de cy-près se-mé de blanches
cresc.
ff>pp
Très lent.
pier-res.
Dieu, pour vous re-po-ser, dans le désert du
rit.
pp

temps, Comme des o-a-sis a mis les ci-me-tiè - - res. Couchez -
vous, et dor - mez, Voy-a - geurs ha-le - tants!
pp
p
pp
p
pp

Le temps des lilas
[The time of lilacs]

Closing section of "La mort de l'amour"—Part 3 of *Poème de l'amour et de la mer,* Op. 19 (1886) • Poem by Maurice Bouchor

le temps des œil_lets aus - si.
M. G.
Le vent a chan - gé, les cieux sont mo - ro - ses, Et nous
augmentez un peu
n'irons plus cou - rir, et cueil - lir Les li - las en fleur et les bel_les
f
ro - ses; Le prin temps est triste et ne peut fleu_rir.
p

en pressant un peu
plus f
p
Plus animé
f
Oh! joy - eux et doux prin - temps de l'an - né - e, Qui vins, l'an pas - sé, nous en - so - leil - ler,
mf
17
f

No - tre fleur d'a - mour est si bien fa - né - - - e,
cresc.
moins f
cresc.
ff
f
Las!
f
que ton bai - ser ne peut l'e - veil - ler!
f
mf simplement
3
Et toi, que fais-tu?
p
mf

p
pas de fleurs é - clo - ses,
Point de gai so - leil
ni d'om - bra - ges
p
pp
p au premier mouvement
frais;
pp
Lent
pp
Le temps des li - las
et le temps des ro - ses
Avec notre a - mour
est mort
mf
à ja - mais.
pp
pp
ppp

Serre chaude

[Greenhouse]

No. 1 (1896) from *Serres chaudes,* Op. 24 • Poem by Maurice Maeterlinck

Et tout ce qu'il y a sous vo_tre cou_
-po - le! Et dans mon â - -
- - me en vos a_na_lo_gies!
retenu
Ier mouvt
retenu
Ier mouvt
p
mp

Les pensées d'u_ne prin - ces_se qui a faim,
L'ennui d'un ma_te - lot dans le dé_sert,
U_ne mu_si - que de cui - vreaux fe_nê - tres des in - cu -
- ra - - - - bles.

mf
Al - lez aux an - gles les plus tiè - des!
p
On di - rait u - ne femme é - va - nou - ie un jour de moisson,
Il y a des postil - lons dans la cour de l'hos - pi - ce.
Au loin

passe un chasseur d'é - lan
de - ve - nu in - fir - mier
Ex - a - mi - nez au clair de lu -
moins f
- ne.
Oh!
rien n'yest à sa
en di - mi -
pla - ce.
nu ant
On dirait u - ne fol - le
p

devant les ju-ges,
Un na-vi-re de guerre
à pleines voi - les
Sur un ca - nal
en animant et en augmentant
Des oi-seaux de nuit sur des
lis
Un
glas vers midi
(Là - bàs
sous ces clo - ches!)
Une é - ta pe de ma-

-la-des dans la prai-rie Une o-deur d'é-
1er mouvt
-ther un jour de so-leil
ff
f
Mon Dieu!
Mon
en retenant

Dieu!
dim.
Plus lent (grave)
Quand au - rons - nous la pluie Et la
p
neige Et le vent dans la ser - - -
mf
- re!
pp

Serre d'ennui

[Hothouse of ennui]

No. 2 (1893) from *Serres chaudes,* Op. 24 • Poem by Maurice Maeterlinck

bleus de lan_gueur! Cet en_nui
mf
bleu com_me la ser_re, Où l'on voit clo_ses à tra_
p
_vers Les vi_tra_ges pro_fonds et verts, Cou_ver_tes de
lune et de ver_re Les gran_des
m.g.
mf

vé - gé - ta - ti - ons Dont l'ou - bli noc - tur - ne s'al-
-lon - ge, Im - mo - bi - le - ment
Comme un son - ge Sur les ro - ses des pas - si -
-ons. Où de l'eau très len - te s'é -

-lè - ve
En mé-lant la lune et le
ciel
En un san-glot glauque
é - ter -
-nel
Mo - no - to - ne - ment
comme un rê - - - ve.
p
mf
mp
pp
p
pp

Lassitude

No. 3 (1893) from *Serres chaudes,* Op. 24 • Poem by Maurice Maeterlinck

son - ge su-per-be, Ils re - gar - dent rê-veurs
p
com-me des chiens dans l'her - be,
La fou - le des bre-bis gri - ses à l'ho-ri-zon Brou-ter le clair de
lune é - pars sur le ga -

-zon.
Aux ca-res - ses du
mp
p
ciel, va - gue com-me leur vie, In-dif-fé-
-rent et sans u - ne flam - me d'en-vi - e
Pour ces ro - ses de joie é -

clo - ses sous leurs pas
p
Et ce long cal - me vert qu'ils ne com -
p
-prennent pas.

Fauves las

[Wearied beasts]

No. 4 (1896) from *Serres chaudes,* Op. 24 • Poem by Maurice Maeterlinck

et les yeux mi - clos Par - mi les
feuil - les ef - feuil - lées, Les chiens jau - nes de mes pé -
- chés, Les hyè - nes lou - ches de mes hai - nes
Et sur l'en - nui pâ - le des plai - nes Les li -

-ons de l'a-mour cou-chés!
En l'impuis-san-ce de leur
p
rêve Et lan-gui-des sous la lan-
mf
-gueur De leur ciel morne et sans cou-

-leur
El-les re-gar-de-
-ront
sans
trè
-
ve
Les
bre-
-bis
des
ten-ta
-
ti
-
ons
S'é-loi-
-gner
len
-
-
tes
une
à

u - ne
En l'im - mo - bi - le
clair de lu - ne
Mes im - mo -
-bi - les pas - si - ons!
mf
p
pp

Oraison

[A prayer]

No. 5 (1895) from *Serres chaudes,* Op. 24 • Poem by Maurice Maeterlinck

Voy_ez aus _ si ma las_si _ tu _ de,
dim.
La lune é _ teinte et l'au _ be noi _ re; Et fé_con_
_dez ma so_li _ tude En l'ar_ro _ sant de vo_tre gloi _ re.
Ou _ vrez-moi, Sei _ gneur, vo _ tre

mf
voie, E - clai - rez mon â - me
mf
las - se Car la tris - tes - se de ma
p
p
joie Sem - ble de l'her - be sous la
gla - ce.
p
pp

Les heures
[The hours]

No. 1 (1896) from *Trois lieder,* Op. 27 • Poem by Camille Mauclair

Où, a-vec un som-bre souri - re,
El-les ten - dent, une à u - ne,
Les mains qui mè - nent à mou - rir;
Et cer -
-tains, blè - - mes sous la lune
Aux yeux d'i - ris sans souri - - re,
Sa -
-chant que l'heure est de mourir,
Don - nent leurs mains une à
p
mf
p

p
u - - ne
Et tous s'en vont dans
l'ombre et dans la lu - ne Pour s'a-lan-guir et puis mou-rir
A - vec les Heu - res une à u - - - ne, Les
Heu - - res au pâ - - le sou - ri - - re.
pp

Ballade

No. 2 (1896) from *Trois lieder,* Op. 27 • Poem by Camille Mauclair

-dus, Puis, s'en sont al-lés dans le vent a-mer
S'en sont al-lés jus-qu'aux chaumiè-res Qui
dor-ment au bord de la mer;
Et ils ont dit qu'étaient per-dus Les
an-ges at-ten-dus.
S'en sont al-lés aux clochers des é-
p
(♯)
mf
p

mf
_gli _ ses Qui chan _ tent se_lon la bri _ se, Et ils ont
dit qu'étaient per_dus Les vai_seaux at _ ten_dus.
pp
pp
Et la
nuit les enfants é _ tran_ges Ont vu les ai_les des an _ ges Com_me des vaisseaux flot_
_ter au ciel, Ont vu des voi _ les comme des ai _ les Pla _

- ner vers les é - toi - les.
Et mê - lant les
ai - les, les voi - les, Et les navires et les an - ges, Ils ont pri - é,
les en - fants frê - - les, Dans une i - gno - ran - ce
blan - - che.
retenu

Les couronnes

[Garlands]

No. 3 (1896) from *Trois lieder,* Op. 27 • Poem by Camille Mauclair

ro - se d'au - tom - ne.
La pim - pre - nelle est pour son
p
â - me, La vigne est pour l'a - mu - ser, La
ro - se à qui voudra l'ai - mer.
sfz
mp
Beau che-va-lier!
retenu
1er Mouvt
p
Beau che-valier!
très retenu

1er Mouvt
p
Mais il ne pas - se plus per - son - ne, Et la fil -
- lette aux yeux cer - nés A lais - sé tom - ber les cou -
- ron - - - - nes.

Chanson de clowns

[Song of the clowns]

No. 1 (1890) from *Chansons de Shakespeare,* Op. 28

Text by Maurice Bouchor, based on "Come away, come away, death"

from William Shakespeare's *Twelfth Night,* Act II, Scene iv

cier - ges Dans un cer - cueil de noir cy - près .
cresc.
poco f
Qu'on m'en se-ve - lis - se loin d'el - le Dans le blê-me lin - ceul cou -
p sost.
-vert de bran-ches d'if, Qui, par-ta - geant mon sort, a-mi sûr mais tar -
-dif, Du moins me res-te-ra fi - dè - - le.
pp

Que pas u - ne fleur, u - ne pau-vre fleur Sur ma
tom - be ne soit se - mée; Pour
moi que nul a - mi que nul - le voix ai - mée
N'ait des pa - ro - les de dou - leur.
p
dim.
p
pp

Que je sois seul a - vec mes pei - nes, Et lais - sez au dé - sert blan - chir mes os - se - ments,
De peur que sur ma tombe, he - lás ! les vrais a - mants Ne ver - sent trop de lar - mes vai - nes.
p
cresc.
poco f
p
pp
8

Chanson d'amour

[Song of love]

No. 2 (1891) from *Chansons de Shakespeare,* Op. 28

Text by Maurice Bouchor, based on "Take, O! take those lips away" from William Shakespeare's *Measure for Measure,* Act IV, Scene i

yeux que le ciel de mai prend pour l'au - ro - re Ces
retenu
yeux qui ren - draient le ma - tin ja - loux Loin de
moi, loin de moi ces lè - vres que j'a -
- dore Et dont le men - songe hé - las! fut si
3

doux.
Mais si mal-gré tout ma douleur te
tou - - che Ah! rends -
moi, rends - moi mes bai -

-sers,
Sceaux d'a - mour qui
fu - rent po - sés En vain sur tes
yeux tes yeux et ta
bou - - che.
f
p

Chanson d'Ophélia
[Ophelia's song]

No. 3 (1896) from *Chansons de Shakespeare,* Op. 28
Text by Maurice Bouchor, based on "He is dead and gone, lady"
from William Shakespeare's *Hamlet,* Act IV, Scene v

Sur le lin_ceul de neige à plei_nes mains se_mées, Mil_le
pp
fleurs par_fu_mées, A_vant d'al_ler sous terre a_vec lui sans re_
_tour Dans leur jeu_nesse é_pa_nou_ie Ont bu, comme u_ne fraî_che
pluie, Les lar_mes du sin_cère a_mour.
p
dim.
pp

La chanson bien douce

[A very sweet song]

No. 1 (1910) from *Deux poèmes,* Op. 34 • Poem by Paul Verlaine

-gere: Un fris - son d'eau sur de la
mous - se.
La voix vous fut con - nue et chè -
- - re, Mais à présent elle est voi -

-lée Comme u - ne veu - ve dé - so - lée
Pourtant comme elle en-co - re fiè -
-re Et dans les longs plis de son voi - le Qui pal-pite aux bri-ses d'au-
-tom - ne Cache et montre au

cœur qui s'é_ton - - ne La vé _ ri _
té comme une é _ toi _ le.
El _ le dit, la voix re _ con _ nue Que la bon _
té c'est no _ tre vie Que de la
3
3
3
3

haine et de l'envie Rien ne res - te, la
mort ve - nue.
Accueillez la voix qui per - sis - te Dans son na - ïf é - pi - tha -

-la - - - me
Al-lez, rien n'est meil-leur à l'â -
- me Que de faire une â - me moins
tris - te. Elle est en peine

et de pas-sa-ge L'â - me qui souf - fre sans co-
-lè - - re
Et com-me sa mo-
-rale est clai - re...
E-cou-
-tez la chanson bien sage.
m.g.

Cantique à l'épouse

[A canticle for the wife]

No. 1 (1896) from *Deux mélodies*, Op. 36 • Poem by Albert Jounet

Le crépus_cu - le fée - ri_que t'en_vi_ronne d'un feu ro - se
Viens me chan_ter un can_ti - que Beau comme u_ne som_bre
ro - se
ou plu - tôt ne chante
pas
Viens te cou - cher sur mon cœur

Lais - se - moi bai - ser tes bras
3
Pâ - les com - me l'aube en fleur La
en pressant
Plus animé
nuit de tes yeux m'at - ti - - re.
Nuit frémissan - te, mys - ti - - que,

en revenant au Ier mouvt
Dou - ce com_me ton sou_rire heu_reux et mé_lan_co_
Ier mouvt
_li - que
Et sou_dain la pro_fon_deur du pas_sé re_li_gi_
retenu Ier mouvt
_eux, Le mys_tère et la grandeur De notre a_mour sé_ri_

-eux.
s'ouvre
au
fond
de nos
pen-
-sées
Comme u-ne vallée
immen-
se
où des fo-
-rêts
délaissées
Rê-vent dans
un
grand
si-
len-
ce.
p

Dans la forêt du charme et de l'enchantement

[In the forest of charm and enchantment]

No. 2 (1898) from *Deux mélodies*, Op. 36 • Poem by Jean Moréas

p
-ment
Sous vos sombres che - ve - lu - res, pe-ti-tes
fées Dans la fo - rêt du charme
et de l'en-chan - te - ment
p

Dans la fo - rêt du charme et des mer -
- veil - leux ri - tes
mf
gnô - mes com - pa - tis - sants, pen - dant que je dor -
- mais, de vo - tre main, hon - nê - tes

gnô - mes vous m'of - fri - tes un scep - tre
cresc.
d'or
hé - las!
f
pen - dant
dim.
que je dor - mais
dim.
p

retenu
plus lent
J'ai su depuis ce
p
temps que c'est mi - rage et leur -
- re Les scep - tres d'or et les chan -
- sons dans la fo - rêt,
Pour - tant

comme un en-fant cré-du - le, je les
pleu - re et je voudrais dor-mir
en-cor dans la fo - rêt Qu'im-
-por - - - - te si je
mf
f
f

sais que c'est mi - rage et
mf
leur - - - re.
f sonore
dimi - - - nu - - - en - - - do
p

Chanson perpétuelle

[Perpetual chanson]

Op. 37 (1898) • Poem by Charles Cros

[Piano part transcribed by the composer from the orchestral original]

-lé.
Vents, que vos plainti - ves ru-
un peu plus f
p
-meurs, Que vos chants, rossignols charmeurs, Aillent lui di - re
que je meurs.
p
Ped.
expressif

très simple
très peu retenu
Le premier soir qu'il vint i - ci Mon â - me fut à sa mer -
très peu retenu
1er mouvt
- ci;
De fier - té je n'eus plus sou -
1er mouvt
plus f
mp
- ci. Mes regards étaient pleins d'a - veux, Il me prit dans ses bras ner -
pp
- veux Et me bai - sa près des che - veux
cresc.
f
tr

mf
p
J'en eus un grand fré_mis_se_ment.
Et puis
dim.
en
en diminuant
je ne sais plus comment
Il est de_ve_nu mon a_
diminuant toujours
pp
_mant.
Je lui di_sais:
Tu m'aime_
pp
un peu moins lent
_ras
Aussi long_temps
que tu pour_ras.
pp un peu moins lent

retenu
1er mouvt
mf
Je ne dormais bien qu'en ses bras
Mais lui,
retenu
1er mouvt
sfz
p
p
sentant son cœur é_teint,
S'en est al_lé l'au_tre ma_tin
f
Sans moi
p
dans un pa_ys loin_tain
cresc.
mf
f
Puisque je n'ai plus mon a_
sfz
sfz
sfz
p

p
-mi
Je mourrai dans l'é-tang par-mi les
dim.
p
plus p
fleurs sous le flot en-dor-mi;
m.d.
dimin.
sempre
pp m.g.
m.d.
p
Sur le bord ar-ri-vée, au vent Je di-rai son nom
m.g.
en rê-vant Que là je l'at-ten-dis sou-

-vent
Et comme en un linceul do-ré, Dans
marqué
p
mes cheveux défaits, au gré Du vent je m'a-ban-don-ne-rai.
retenu
1er mouvt
en diminuant
pp
Les bonheurs pas-sés ver-se-ront Leur dou-ce lu-
sfz
en
-eur sur mon front Et les joncs verts m'en-la-ce-
diminuant
pp

END OF EDITION